# SHOWDOWN IN THE MIDDLE EAST

George E. Vandeman

Pacific Press Publishing Association
Boise, Idaho
Oshawa, Ontario, Canada

Scripture passages in this book credited to sources other than the King James Version are as follows:

N.I.V. From the *New International Version,* copyright © by the New York Bible Society International 1978.

Cover illustration and book design by Tim Mitoma

Litho in United States of America



ISBN 0-8163-0392-4

96 95 94 93 92 91

# Contents

# Showdown in the Middle East

Once upon a time, according to the legend, a scorpion came to the Jordan River and wanted to get across. But he couldn't swim. He saw a frog there on the shore, and he said, "Dear frog, would you kindly carry me across the river?"

But the frog dived into the river as he said, "I wouldn't dream of it. I know you. You might sting me."

"Oh, no," said the scorpion, "have no fear. If I did that while we were crossing the river, then we would both perish."

That reassured the frog. So he came back to shore and said, "Hop on my back, then, and I will give you a ride across."

So the scorpion hopped on the frog's back and they started across. But in midstream the scorpion suddenly stung the frog. As the two were sinking beneath the waves, the frog cried out, "Scorpion, why did you do that? Now we shall both die!"

And the scorpion replied, "Well, this is the Middle East!"

Yes, that's the Middle East. Confused. Puzzling. Explosive. Unreasonable. A land of changing alliances where the frog today may be the scorpion tomorrow.

Ready to sting at the slightest provocation. Even if the whole Middle East should sink!

Such is the strange reasoning—or lack of reasoning—in that part of the world. And it is no secret that the peace and security of the whole planet is tied to what happens in the Middle East.

Why is this? Why will a great superpower wink at aggression in some other part of the world, but bristle with threats at the slightest approach toward the Persian Gulf?

What do these mysterious lands have that others so desperately want? Oil. It wouldn't take much of a prophet to predict that a military showdown in the Middle East would be over oil.

Complicating the problem, and greatly increasing its explosiveness, is the fact that the conflict, more and more, has taken on religious overtones. A secular power will coldly calculate the cost of its moves. But when people's first loyalty is to its religion, there may be no calculation at all.

It was bad enough when Arabs claimed lands as their homes because they had lived there for thousands of years—and Israelis claimed the same lands because God gave them to their ancestors in the days of Abraham.

But how could you deal with a people that didn't mind being stung by the scorpion, that didn't mind sinking, that wouldn't mind dying in "serving God"? What does a nation of would-be martyrs care about international law, world opinion, or military threats?

On the other hand, would it help if we better understood the world of Islam—the background and perspective from which the Muslim views the West?

The forces of an Islamic revival, which dominated the

news in the late seventies, seemed to Westerners like the return of medieval barbarity. No wonder news commentators could not understand the closing of bars, casinos, and cinemas, and the execution of prostitutes and other moral offenders.

But conservative Christians should have understood. For they frown upon many of the same sins. Yet, they do not deal with offenders so harshly. Flogging a criminal for some petty offense, amputating a hand for theft, or shooting a girl for immoral conduct seems far too severe.

But the truth is that the permissiveness of the West, the failure of Christianity to live up to its own moral standards, is a big part of the problem. The Muslim often feels vastly superior to the Christian. After all, why should America tell a Muslim country what to do—when American Christians worship "three gods," bow to idols, and frequently get drunk?

Let me illustrate. An Australian couple stopped over in an Arab city. They approached a local businessman in the lobby of the hotel and asked where they might see a belly dance. The businessman frowned and looked them over carefully. He noticed the woman wore no wedding ring. Obviously, to him, they were simply immoral Europeans out to enjoy the worst of life.

So what did the businessman do? Motivated by both honor and hospitality, he invited the couple to dinner with his family in a good restaurant. In that way he helped the Australians to avoid such evils as dance shows.

Another instance. A man approached a fruit vendor selling melons from a cart. He found an overripe Crenshaw melon that smelled delicious and wanted to buy it. It had a bruised spot, however. You would expect the fruit vendor to be delighted to get rid of a melon that would soon rot. Instead, he absolutely refused to sell it, and finally threw it on the ground.

A few minutes later, as he wandered on through the marketplace, this same man felt a tap on his shoulder, and half a cucumber was thrust into his bag. A merchant had charged him too much for some cucumbers and was correcting his mistake.

Said a devout Muslim who had been reading *Newsweek* magazine, with its recital of crime and corruption, "I don't understand why you Americans send all these missionaries over here!"

Perhaps now we can understand just a little better the label "Satan America."

But understanding does not make the Middle East less explosive. Nor does it make its problems easier to untangle. The whole area sits upon a pool of oil. And no one knows which fuse will ignite it first!

When we turn to the area of Bible prophecy, particularly prophecies about Israel, a great deal of confusion still exists. There are sincere Bible students who have constructed from Scripture a series of end-time events that they believe are about to take place in Israel, centering in Jerusalem and including the building of another temple. They are carefully watching events in Israel, and estimating the nearness of our Lord's return accordingly.

The problem is that there are many, many Bible predictions about Israel. But many of them were conditional upon what ancient Israel did or did not do. Many of the promises clearly contain an "if." *If* the people were loyal to God, *if* they remained faithful to Him, He would do certain things for them.

But when Israel as a nation failed to carry out its

appointed mission as a light to the world, when it forfeited its position as a chosen people by the rejection of Christ as the Messiah, a change in relationship came in. The promises made to Israel on the condition of obedience could not be fulfilled to them. They would now be reserved for spiritual Israel—for Jews and Gentiles alike who have accepted Christ. And most of these promises will find fulfillment only in the future life, in the earth made new.

One of the reasons that Jesus was rejected by His own people is that the religious leaders of His day had misapplied Scripture. They had taken scriptures that apply to our Lord's second coming in glory and forcibly applied them to their own time. Then they rejected Jesus because He did not fit their mistaken assumptions, because He did not come as a King.

That same sort of thing may happen today. There is danger that we should become so engrossed with our assumptions about Jerusalem—which likely are mistaken assumptions—that we are completely surprised, taken unaware, by the return of our Lord in the skies!

This, however, is not to deny that the Middle East, from the beginning, has been the focal point of the history of this planet. I wonder if you realize that almost every great event, so far as the relation of this planet to its God is concerned, has centered, or will center, in the Middle East. And every major confrontation between God and His enemies, every major showdown, has been in that part of the world. The final showdown just ahead of us, though it will involve the whole planet, will still have a focal point in the Middle East.

There is no way that we can know the location of Eden, the garden home that the Creator prepared for our first parents. The book of Genesis tells us that a river flowed out from Eden and divided into four. The names of two of these rivers, the Tigris and the Euphrates, have caused some to speculate that the Garden of Eden was in the Mesopotamian Valley. However, the entire surface of the planet was so drastically altered at the time of Noah's Flood that it is impossible to tie any post-Flood locality to pre-Flood days.

After the Flood, however, we are not left to speculation. We are told definitely that the ark came to rest "upon the mountains of Ararat." Genesis 8:4.

It is no surprise, then, that recorded history seems to radiate from that area.

Since those early days, many have been the enormously important political and religious showdowns centering in the explosive Middle East. In these pages we will focus on three. Perhaps the most important of all Middle East showdowns.

Approximately 1500 years, B.C., along the banks of the Nile, a head-on confrontation took place between God and an Egyptian king who was as stubborn and as unpredictable as any ayatollah!

Then in the days of Elijah came a second showdown, with the prophet Elijah standing alone against 450 prophets of Baal, the sun-god. That is one of the most thrilling stories of all time.

The third major showdown is yet to come. We call it Armageddon. And already we can feel its fiery breath!

The first two confrontations happened in the Middle East. The third, Armageddon, will also have its focal point there.

Add to this the fact that Jesus, the Son of God, when He came to live among us, was born, lived, and was crucified in the Middle East. From there He ascended to heaven. When He returns to take His people to the home prepared for them, His coming will be witnessed worldwide (Revelation 1:7), and He will catch His people up into the cloud of angels without Himself touching the earth (1 Thessalonians 4:16, 17).

But when, after a thousand years (Revelation 20:4, last part), Jesus returns to this earth with His people, again the point of contact will be the Middle East. We are told that His feet will stand upon the Mount of Olives, just outside Jerusalem (Zechariah 14:4). The mountain will become a great plain on which the New Jerusalem, moved from heaven to earth (Revelation 21:2, 10), will rest. And it is there, outside the city, that rebellion will meet its final judgment and sin will be no more. Revelation 20:9.

Such is the story of the Middle East, from start to finish. It might even be called the navel of this planet, the point of attachment to its Creator.

The great confrontations between God and those who oppose His designated people (which in these pages we shall view in more detail) are all a part of a great controversy that began in heaven. It began when heaven's highest angel challenged the government of God, in particular the authority of Christ. Lucifer, that exalted angel, proud of his own beauty, had determined to gain for himself the place of Christ, the Son of God. "How art thou fallen from heaven, O Lucifer, son of the morning! how art thou cut down to the ground, which didst weaken the nations! For thou hast said in thine heart, I will ascend into heaven, I will exalt my throne above the stars of God: . . . I will ascend above the heights of the clouds; I will be like the most High." Isaiah 14:12-14.

The conflict, primarily, is between Christ and Lucifer, now called Satan. But it also involves the angels loyal to Christ and the angels who rebelled with

Lucifer. For we read, "There was war in heaven: Michael [Christ] and his angels fought against the dragon; and the dragon fought and his angels, and prevailed not; neither was their place found any more in heaven. And the great dragon was cast out, that old serpent, called the Devil, and Satan, which deceiveth the whole world: he was cast out into the earth, and his angels were cast out with him." Revelation 12:7-9.

This planet, then, became the theater of conflict. And now every member of the human race is involved. We are involved because our first parents, by open disobedience, involved us.

It is important to remember, then, as the controversy winds up to its final climax, that the participants are still the same. The angels of God and the angels of Satan, though invisible to us, are still in conflict. Said the apostle Paul, "We wrestle not against flesh and blood, but against principalities, against powers, against the rulers of the darkness of this world, against spiritual wickedness in high places." Ephesians 6:12.

Only as we remember the nature of this conflict and who the participants are—only then will we be able to understand what is happening today. For the book of Revelation tells us clearly that Satan's angels, his angels-turned-demons, are stirring up the nations to an anger that will soon culminate in Armageddon.

We shall discover, as we look at these three great showdowns, some most striking parallels. In all three the issues are the same. All three are a challenge to God's authority. In all three there is an involvement with sun worship. Even in our day? Yes, even in our day. In all three there is an attack upon God's law. In all three the cherished objects of false worship are unmasked completely, shown to be incapable of saving their followers. And in all three a clear line is drawn between those who serve God and those who serve Him not.

In our day, in the eyes of many, it is coming to be considered something of a crime to discriminate between those who do right and those who do wrong. But God discriminates. He makes a clear distinction—so clear that no man can miss it!

And then, after looking closely at the three great showdowns, we shall discover that the life of Jesus, particularly as it led to the cross, was the greatest showdown of all. For Calvary was a head-on collision with the invisible forces of Satan. And it was Satan who lost!

Recently I heard of a man, a Cambodian I believe, who found a Bible. It was a Bible from which the first six chapters of Genesis and the last ten chapters of Revelation were missing. And I was thinking. I was thinking that if the situation had been reversed—if he had *only* the first six chapters of Genesis and the last ten chapters of Revelation—he still could have discovered the way to Christ and to life. He still could look to the future with hope and confidence.

In the early pages he would have seen man created in the image of God, with limitless possibilities. And then the intrusion of an enemy. Man's tragic fall. But immediately the promise of a Saviour. Yet, in spite of that divine provision, the increase of rebellion—until God found it necessary to destroy almost the entire human race in a global flood.

Turning to the final chapters of Revelation, that man with his abbreviated Bible would see that the conflict is not over. He would see it accelerating to a fearful climax as the armies of men and of demons make war with the Lamb. But he sees the Lamb victorious. He sees a new heaven and a new earth—and an endless day where heartache and tears and sin and death itself are forever gone. And he is led to pray with John who wrote the book, "Even so, come, Lord Jesus!"

In September of 1977 a crowd of fifty thousand Christians assembled in Kansas City. The speaker, sensing the mood of his audience, lifted his Bible high into the air as he said, "If you sneak a peek at the back of the Book, Jesus wins!" And the great crowd roared their approval with ten minutes of cheering and applause.

Yes, friend! Jesus will win! And you and I can be on the winning side if we choose. Sin and rebellion and heartache and death are on the way out—all because of Jesus. Life, never-ending life, can be yours if you want it. You can choose it now—by choosing Him!

# Confrontation on the Nile

In the court of the king he had been educated to take the throne of the mightiest nation on earth. At forty years of age he was a brilliant military leader, a favorite with the armies of Egypt. The world was before him, with the flattering prospect of wealth and fame and power. And he turned it all down!

You see, Moses was not an Egyptian. He was a member of the enslaved Hebrew race. And Moses had a secret. Angels had told him that he had been chosen by God to deliver his people from their life of slavery and oppression.

You recall the story. Joseph, the favorite son of Jacob, had been sold to a passing caravan by his jealous brothers. He soon found himself in Egypt, alone, far from the comforts and the favorable influences of home.

But Joseph remained true to his God. In God's providence he was elevated from prison to become prime minister of Egypt, second only to the king. The king, in a time of severe famine, encouraged Joseph to bring his father's large family to Egypt, where they were assigned the land of Goshen, a choice section of Egypt—all a thrilling story.

But when Joseph died, and the friendly king died, everything changed. The Hebrews became a nation of slaves, living under the most severe oppression.

At the time of Moses' birth, the reigning king, determined to slow the growth of the despised people, had decreed that all male Hebrew babies be killed. But God's plans cannot be altered by the decree of a king. The mother of Moses determined to spare her child. One day the king's daughter found him floating in a basket on the Nile. It was love at first sight. And that is how Moses, a Hebrew, came to be educated for the throne of mighty Egypt.

God was not unaware of the desperate plight of His people. He had promised to bring them back to their own land. And now the time was near.

Moses, knowing the role of leadership that God had assigned to him, guarded his affections. He must not let himself become too attached to his foster mother, to the king, or to the luxury of the royal court. For all these ties were soon to be broken.

It is not strange that Moses, brilliant military leader that he was, assumed that he was to lead his people out of Egypt by force. He expected to take command of the Hebrews and lead them in a revolt against the nation that oppressed them. He saw the providence of God in the preparation he had received. Moses, in his own eyes, was ready. He was confident. Perhaps even a trace of cockiness.

But Moses, in God's eyes, was *not ready at all.* And suddenly, as the result of a foolish, impulsive act, he was fleeing Egypt for his life. And he ended up in the land of Midian—herding sheep!

Did Moses pout? Was his pride wounded? Did he say, "Look, God! All this education, all this training, all this military background, all this perfect preparation—and You want me to herd sheep?''

No. Moses did not pout. Not for forty days or forty weeks but for forty years, Moses let God teach him, change him, and mold him. Out under the open skies he learned patience and compassion until his character was much like that of Jesus who was to come.

Much of what he had learned in Egypt must be unlearned. Its attractions must fade. As the years passed, even the language of Egypt, no longer used, became rusty. And when at last, after forty years, Moses met God at the burning bush, every trace of cockiness was gone. Now he was willing to depend upon God instead of himself. Now he was ready!

The time had come. God's people would be delivered. But God would accomplish that deliverance in a way that would pour contempt on human pride. He asked Moses to return to Egypt not as a military general, but as a humble shepherd, with only a rod in his hand. And God would make that rod a symbol of His power!

And what did Moses say? Was he eager for the job? No. He offered such a string of protests that God finally became annoyed with him. ''Lord, I can't do it. You've got the wrong man. What would I say to the king? Nobody would believe me. I've never been an eloquent speaker anyway, and I haven't spoken Egyptian for forty years. Lord, please send somebody else!''

But God told Moses that his brother, Aaron, who had remained in Egypt, was now on his way to meet him. Aaron could speak for him. And so it was that Moses and Aaron, with only a shepherd's rod, were soon on their way to one of the greatest confrontations of all time!

Yes, it is the story of a king more stubborn and unpredictable than any ayatollah. Of magicians who could produce frogs but couldn't get rid of them. And a quiet, unassuming man who brought the mightiest nation on earth to its knees with nothing but a shepherd's rod—and an invincible faith gained out under the stars, herding sheep!

Imagine, if you can, two strangers, members of a despised race, walking shoulders squared into the palace of the king. No machine guns. No bodyguards. Nothing but a shepherd's rod. Walking right into the king's oval office and telling him they have a message for him from the God of heaven. What a laugh! A good little story to wind up the six o'clock news!

This is how the confrontation began: "Moses and Aaron went to Pharaoh and said, 'This is what the Lord, the God of Israel, says: "Let my people go." ' " Exodus 5:1, N.I.V.

And the king didn't even stop to think it over. He responded immediately, "Who is the Lord, that I should obey him and let Israel go? I do not know the Lord and I will not let Israel go." Verse 2, N.I.V.

I think the king was enjoying this. Something to break up his humdrum day. Yet he sensed that here was no trivial encounter. You see, the king was worshiped as a representative of Egypt's god. He considered that he was a sort of god himself. So this would really be a confrontation between two gods. And of course he knew who would win. He was eager to show up these two daring imposters and their God, whoever He was!

God had asked one thing of the king: "Let My people go!" And the king had said, "No!"

About all that resulted from that first encounter was that the Hebrews were oppressed more than ever.

Moses now had two problems. The king wouldn't listen to him. Neither would his own people. For now they blamed him for making their situation worse.

But God sent Moses and Aaron back to the king to repeat His command, "Let My people go!" This time the king demanded a miracle, something to prove the power of the God of Israel. So as God had previously directed, Aaron stretched out his rod, and it became a serpent.

That was nothing. Just a little magic. The king called in his magicians. They turned their rods into serpents too—that is, they *appeared* to. Even Satan, who was working through the magicians, could not actually create life.

Then Aaron's rod swallowed up their rods. But the king was not greatly impressed. These men knew a trick his men didn't. That was all.

But God would soon silence the king's proud boasting. He would show up the helplessness of the senseless deities that men worship. This is something He would do in all three of the major confrontations with His enemies. He would begin now with the Nile—the sacred Nile. For the overflowing river, the source of food and wealth for all Egypt, was worshiped as a god.

The next morning, at God's direction, Moses and Aaron met the king at the river's edge. The proud ruler was told what was about to take place. Then Aaron stretched out his rod and struck the water of the sacred stream. It was turned to blood. There was blood everywhere in Egypt. But the king was not greatly troubled by this first judgment of God—especially since his magicians could also turn water to blood. If they knew how to turn blood back to water, it would be more helpful. Maybe he should send them back to the university for a refresher course on the latest in magic.

Seven days passed. Again the king was warned. God would not take him by surprise. This time it was frogs—frogs everywhere, in the houses, in the bedrooms. They even got into the bread before it was baked. And the palace was not spared.

But what to do now? Egyptians regarded frogs as sacred. They wouldn't think of killing them. Yet the slimy pests became intolerable. And time was running out for the magicians. They had *appeared* to produce frogs too. But they couldn't get rid of them!

The king now had to call for help. He called for Moses and Aaron and said, "Pray to the Lord to take the frogs away from me and my people, and I will let your people go." Exodus 8:8, N.I.V.

You have to smile just a little at Moses' answer. For he said, "I leave to you the honor of setting the time for me to pray for you." Verse 9.

And the king said, "Tomorrow." If only the slimy frogs would go away by themselves before tomorrow, he would be spared the humiliation.

But they didn't. So Moses prayed. And the frogs all died. They were piled into heaps all over Egypt, and the land reeked with the stench of dead frogs.

This was getting unpleasant. It wasn't a joke any more. But as soon as the frogs were gone, the king changed his mind about letting the people go.

You know how it is. "Lord, if You'll just get me out of this mess, I'll serve You the rest of my life." "Lord, if You'll just bring this plane down safe, I'll do anything You say." "Lord, if You'll just heal me, I'll promise—"

But the promises aren't always kept!

The next judgment was lice—lice everywhere. And now the magicians were frightened. This one they could not duplicate. They were up against more than magic. They were honest enough to acknowledge, "This is the finger of God." But the king was unmoved.

God had done in Egypt what He would do in the great showdown in the days of the prophet Elijah—and what He will yet do as Armageddon breaks about us. He lets Satan and his agents work their miracles first. Then He works His. And the miracles of men and demons end up looking like silly tricks!

Well, next time, Pharaoh, it will be flies. Big, venomous flies with a painful bite. Flies everywhere—inside and outside. But next time God will begin to make a difference between those who serve Him and those who don't. For there will be no flies in the land of Goshen, where the Hebrews live.

So Egypt was ruined by the flies. And the king was impressed. He agreed to let the people go and worship their God—if they would just stay within the borders of Egypt.

But, Pharaoh, don't you know that you can't limit God? You can't set borders for Him! God has promised to bring His people *out* of Egypt. He has more in mind for them than just to linger on the border of freedom!

"Very well," said the king. "You can go out in the desert and worship your God. But don't go very far. And now pray for me."

So Moses prayed. And suddenly the flies were gone. Not a fly remained. And what did Pharaoh do? He did what he had done every time. He changed his mind as soon as the flies were gone. "But this time also Pharaoh hardened his heart and would not let the people go." Exodus 8:32, N.I.V.

Notice that Pharaoh hardened his own heart. God didn't harden it. God only permitted the king, as He permits every man, to exercise free will. The king, like every other man, was free to say No to God if he chose. But the man who keeps saying No to God is pouring cement into his heart. And if he keeps saying No, the time comes when he doesn't even hear the question. He doesn't even hear the appeal of the Spirit of God. And it isn't God's fault that his heart becomes hard. God is just permitting nature to take its natural course. He is just honoring a man's choice!

Well, the lesser judgments upon Egypt have passed. Each one now will be more severe. The king of Egypt may have thought he was playing games. But he was soon to see that God wasn't!

Next came a terrible stroke upon all the cattle in the fields of Egypt. And they all died—sacred animals and all. But not one animal belonging to the Hebrews died.

The next judgment came still closer. The boils—the terrible boils. Up to now the priests and magicians had encouraged the king in his obstinate course. But now a judgment of God had reached them too. And their foolish claims of power only made them contemptible in the eyes of the people. For all Egypt saw that these proud men could not even protect their own persons.

Again the Hebrews were untouched.

Now would come the hail. And the king was carefully warned. The people could stay in their houses and be safe. But any person who ventured out into the storm would die. The animals brought to shelter would be safe. Those left in the field would die. And again the Hebrews would be safe.

Have the judgments of God upon Egypt seemed a little harsh? Was God too hard on the stubborn king? Does the thought of the plagues of Egypt call up in your mind the picture of a God severe and ruthless, eager to punish—a God lacking in love and compassion?

The very opposite is true. God's dealing with the obstinate king is a striking demonstration of His compassion, of His reluctance to punish. You see, God warned Pharaoh from the beginning that a failure to let His people go would mean the death of the firstborn child in every home in Egypt, including his own. So the king knew what was involved. And God could have sent that judgment first of all and had it over with. Instead He sent frogs and flies and lice—the annoyances and inconveniences that did not threaten life. And God gave the king chance after chance—each time warning him of what was coming next, so that he could escape it if he would.

And someone says, "But was it fair for God to punish the people of Egypt—just because their king was stubborn?"

Yes, God was infinitely fair and infinitely kind. Because the people, in every life-threatening situation, were given the opportunity to escape judgment and to show their faith in the God of heaven by asking shelter in the homes of the Hebrews. And many did just that. Many would leave Egypt along with the Hebrews, choosing to worship their God.

The storm of hail and lightning really frightened the king. He called frantically for Moses and Aaron and cried out, "This time I have sinned. Now pray. We've had enough hail. I'll let the people go!"

And he watched amazed as Moses walked out into the violent storm and passed through it unharmed. When Moses reached the edge of the city, he lifted his hands and prayed, and the storm stopped. And as soon as it stopped, the king changed his mind.

The hail hadn't changed the king's heart. Neither did

the swarms of locusts that came now to devour what was left. And the king's counselors begged him to use reason. "Can't you see that Egypt is ruined? Why don't you let the people go?"

But Pharaoh was still trying to bargain with God, to make some compromise. The men could go—if they would leave the women and children behind. He wanted to be sure they would come back. Finally he agreed to let all the people go—if they would leave their flocks and herds.

But Moses said, "No! Our men go. Our women go. Our children go. Our animals go. Not a hoof stays."

And Pharaoh still says, "No!"

One judgment left—the death of all the firstborn. But God is oh so reluctant to let it fall. He loves the king and his people. How can He give them up? How can He see them destroy themselves by their defiance of their Creator? Pharaoh could have gone down in history as the ruler who willingly acknowledged the God of heaven and let His people go free. And the people of ancient Egypt could have been remembered today as a nation that turned from the worship of false gods to become children of the heavenly King.

And so, in His infinite compassion, God would give all Egypt time to think it over, to realize what they were doing, to see if they really wanted to destroy themselves. Suddenly a deep, oppressive darkness spread over the land. For three days there was light only in the homes of the Israelites. For three days the Egyptians were continually reminded that the sun and the moon, which they had long worshiped as gods, had been turned to blackness by the power of the God of Israel!

Pharaoh still said No!

And then came the night—that terrible night. The

warning was clear. It was sufficient. It could not be misunderstood. At midnight the destroying angel would pass through the land of Egypt. And not a home would be spared the stroke of death. Only in the homes of the Hebrews would there be safety from the fearful death.

And now the Hebrews, too, were to be tested. Up until now it had been enough to be a Hebrew, a descendant of Abraham. But no longer. The destroying angel would spare only those homes where the blood of a lamb was applied to the doorpost as an indication of the faith of those within. It was not enough to be a Hebrew. Not enough to believe in God. They must do something to show their faith!

Oh, friend, do you see the gospel? Do you see how men are saved? It's all there in the blood on the doorpost. It's all there in the blood of a lamb that typified Jesus, the Lamb of God who would let His own blood be shed for the sins of a rebel world.

Do you see? It isn't enough to have the right ancestry. It isn't enough to have Christian parents. It isn't enough to have your name on the church books. And it isn't enough to say, "I believe." There are those who tell you that's all that is necessary—just to believe. And it's true that only Jesus can save. We cannot save ourselves. To believe in Jesus is absolutely essential. But belief isn't worth a thing if it doesn't lead you to do what God asks you to do. It is true that belief is an affair of the heart. *But belief is also something you do!*

The destroying angel passed through the land that terrible night. And a great cry arose from all Egypt. For there was not a home where there was not one dead. Even the palace had not been spared. And now the Hebrews, whom the king had refused to let go, were *driven out*. God had delivered His people—but at what a cost, what a needless cost!

Soon however, the faith of God's people was severely tested. Soon they were camped with the Red Sea before them, a seemingly impossible barrier. To the south a rugged mountain obstructed their progress. Suddenly, in the distance behind them, they saw the flash of armor. They heard the sound of moving chariots. And they knew whose army it was. The king had changed his mind again. And they were trapped. Terror seized the hearts of the people.

But God had led them to that spot so that He might once more show His power to deliver. He directed Moses to stretch out his rod over the sea. As he did so, the waters parted. The people walked through the sea on dry ground, with the water standing like a wall on either side. Safely on the other side, they burst into song!

The foolish Egyptians, with the king himself at their head, tried to follow them. But Moses stretched out his rod again, and the piled-up waters, hissing and roaring, rushed together, swallowing the Egyptian army in their black depths!

But it didn't have to be that way. The king and his army were in that place of fearful danger by their own choice. They had destroyed themselves!

I think you see now that the controversy between Christ and Satan is largely decided in the hearts of individuals. The confrontation on the Nile was between God and a stubborn king. It was also a confrontation between God and each individual Egyptian. Each decided his own fate.

How can any heart be unmoved by what we have just witnessed? For we have been watching, close up, the struggle of a man making a decision. A man who is given chance after chance after chance. But a man who lets love and compassion harden his heart instead of melt it. A man who eventually destroys himself by his own choice. And I say again, It didn't have to be that way. It could have been so different!

How is the controversy being decided in your heart, friend? Do you see the love and compassion expressed in the repeated appeals that come to you? Do you see how reluctant God is to let any harm come to you—how eager He is to save you? Do you see how He longs to see you make the right decision—the decision that means life and happiness forever?

And yet He stands back and lets you make that decision without force or coercion. He will not invade the sacred precincts of the soul where a man decides. Instead, He stands at the door and knocks—and waits while you decide. He's waiting now. He longs to save you. I urge you not to disappoint Him!

# Decision by Fire

False prophets have it easy. They can tell people what they want to hear. They can paint fortune-cookie pictures of the future—with fantasies of knights that come riding and ships that sail out of the horizon loaded with gold. And this, for the prophets, means applause and popularity, an easy road to fame.

False prophets have it easy—until someone comes along and demands proof that they really do have a private line to the sky!

We turn now to the thrilling story of a man who stood alone against 450 false prophets—and demanded a showdown. For three years they had tried unsuccessfully to bring rain from the sky. Could they do better with fire?

And once more the showdown takes place in the sensitive Middle East.

Some years ago it was my privilege to visit Petra, the "rose-red city half as old as time." It took thirty minutes to go through the Siq, with its straight, towering walls—walls so close on either side that at times it seemed you could reach out and touch them both. And suddenly there we were—viewing that ancient mountain fortress, a city carved out of solid rock.

We surveyed it all on horseback and marveled at the wonders of a civilization long gone. But we were looking for the red stairs. They were what we had come to see. For Petra, you see, was an ancient center of sun worship. Arising out of this fabulous city are the red sandstone steps that once led to the high altar of a forbidden god.

As I stood atop those red stairs, it seemed that I could feel the very heartbeat of the great controversy of the ages. I could feel the pulse of this planet's rebellion against its God. And I tried to think how the Creator must have felt as He looked down upon Petra.

But it was not Petra that brought God the greatest heartbreak. What hurt God most was that sun worship had filtered even into Israel. King Ahab had married the wicked Jezebel. The new queen had brought with her the worship of Baal, the sun-god. And the people? The people had followed their weak leaders. *God's own people had gone tramping after other gods!*

It was bad enough, disgraceful enough, that from all over this planet the smoke of strange altars ascended toward heaven. But Israel was not a nation unacquainted with God. Hers was an incomparable heritage. It was Israel that God had delivered from Egyptian slavery. For Israel God had parted the Red Sea—and then let the angry waters roll back upon the Egyptian army. Before Israel the walls of Jericho had fallen. I doubt if there was a child in Israel who didn't know it all by heart. And now it was Israel, with such a heritage, that had forsaken its God!

So it was that in the days of the prophet Elijah the time had come for a confrontation, a showdown. God's people must decide whom they would serve!

Elijah, just as Moses had done in Egypt, walked,

shoulders squared, by the guards and into the presence of the astonished king. The guards seemed not to see him. God's messages have a way of getting through!

And what was the message? Simply this: "As the Lord, the God of Israel, lives, whom I serve, there will be neither dew nor rain in the next few years except at my word." 1 Kings 17:1, N.I.V.

That was all. Elijah turned and walked out before the king could recover from his surprise!

What happened then? For three years and a half there was no dew or rain.

Elijah spent the time in hiding. God directed him first to a brook from which he could drink and where the ravens brought him food. When the brook dried up, God sent him to a widow in a foreign land. She was about to prepare the last bit of food she had for herself and her son—and then die. Elijah, appearing at that moment, asked her to feed him first, promising that her food would last until it rained. And it did!

King Ahab spent the time scouring the country, even the surrounding nations, for Elijah, determined to take his life. Jezebel spent the time planning revenge. Strange—isn't it?—this human tendency to blame the messenger for the message!

As for the 450 prophets of Baal, the sun-god, they spent the time pleading with Baal for rain—to prove Elijah wrong.

And then one day—when three and a half years had passed and the whole land was parched, scorched, and burned by the sun, the object of the people's rebellious worship—the time had come. Elijah simply walked up to a servant of the king, a servant who still worshiped God, and said, "Go tell Ahab I'm here."

The servant was frightened nearly out of his wits.

"No!" he pleaded. "Please don't ask me to do that! God will snatch you away somewhere, you'll be gone, and Ahab will kill me!"

But Elijah assured him that he would talk with the king that very day. The servant went and told Ahab. And Ahab came to meet Elijah.

Imagine what it would be like to stand, unarmed, in the presence of a king who had had a price on your head for three years! But the truth is that Ahab was more scared than Elijah!

"Are you the one who has been troubling Israel?" the king asked awkwardly. And Elijah said, "I haven't been troubling Israel. It's you and your father's house who have troubled Israel by departing from the commandments of God and worshiping Baal."

The king, all this time, has been seeking Elijah's life. But now the prophet stands before him, and he dares not lift a hand against him. It is the prophet, not the king, who is in command. And he gets down to business. He says, "Now summon the people from all over Israel to meet me on Mount Carmel. And bring the four hundred and fifty prophets of Baal." 1 Kings 18:19, N.I.V.

And Ahab, as if he were a servant and Elijah the king, does exactly as he is commanded. He dares not do otherwise!

All over Israel there is apprehension as the word is spread. What terrible judgment will come upon them now?

At the appointed time they gather. The king arrives with the usual pomp and ceremony. And the 450 prophets of Baal march up the mountain in imposing array. And Elijah, standing alone before enemies who would like nothing better than to tear him in pieces, states the issue plainly: "How long will you waver between two opinions? If the Lord is God, follow him; but if Baal is God, follow him." 1 Kings 18:21, N.I.V.

And do you know something? There was not one person in all that crowd who dared to speak up and acknowledge himself a worshiper of the true God!

Elijah then made a proposal. The prophets of Baal should take an animal, prepare it for a sacrifice, put it on the wood, and call upon Baal to send the fire. Then he would do the same and call upon his God. "And the god who answers by fire," he said, "he is God!"

And the people said, "That's fair."

The prophets of Baal would have their chance first. God always lets the false gods work their miracles first—if they can. Outwardly bold and defiant, but with terror in their guilty hearts, the prophets called upon Baal to send fire. They pleaded. They shouted. They leaped and writhed and screamed. They tore their hair and cut their flesh. And nothing happened.

If only they could find a way to light a fire without being detected! But Elijah watched them every second, giving them no chance. Satan would gladly have produced fire to support the claims of his lying agents. But God wouldn't let him!

Finally, late in the day, finding no opportunity to deceive the people, the exhausted prophets retired from the conflict. It was Elijah's turn.

In sharp contrast to the frenzied carrying-on of the prophets, Elijah quietly repairs the broken-down altar where once the God of heaven has been worshiped. The people are tired now of the senseless exhibitions of demonism, and they press near to see what Elijah will do. He places the sacrifice on the altar, around which he has dug a trench. He now commands that the altar be flooded with water. Four barrels of it. Four barrels more. And four barrels more!

If you wonder where they could get all that water in a time of drought, remember that Carmel is close by the Mediterranean Sea.

Then Elijah prays a simple prayer. No senseless shrieks now resound over Carmel. He prays as if he knows God is right there. He has no need to shout.

Hardly is his prayer ended when flames of fire, like brilliant flashes of lightning, descend from heaven. The flames consume the sacrifice, the stones of the altar, even the water in the trench. The mountain is lighted up with the blaze, and the eyes of the people are dazzled.

In the valleys below, where many are watching in suspense, the descent of the fire is clearly seen. The leafless trees do not hide what is happening on the summit.

Those on the mountain now bow in awe before the unseen God who has just demonstrated His power. They dare not continue to look at the fire. They fear that they themselves will be consumed. They are ready now to acknowledge the God they have so disgracefully forsaken, and they cry out as if with one voice, "The Lord, he is the God! The Lord, he is the God!"

The prophets of Baal could have bowed with the people in repentance. But even in the presence of divine glory, they still choose to remain the prophets of Baal. And now God honors their choice. They are ready for destruction. The people, at Elijah's command, seize the prophets who have led them into false worship and spare not one.

What a day! What a victory! What power! What a reformation!

But it was not an edict of the king that turned the

people again to the God of their fathers. Not a piece of national legislation. It was a decision in individual hearts. Each man and woman, each youth, kneeling there on Carmel in the presence of divine power, acknowledged the true God and asked forgiveness for tramping after other gods, after the senseless deities worshiped by the neighboring nations.

So it will be when Armageddon is upon us. Each one of us, individually, must decide which side of the conflict we will be on. When the day of crisis comes, the day of ultimate decision, we may find that we have already made our choice in little decisions along the way—at times like this moment. For sounding down across the centuries into your ears and mine is the clarion call of Elijah, "How long will you waver between two opinions? If the Lord is God, follow him; but if Baal is God, follow him."

But what of Elijah? Was he unduly elated over this landmark victory? Did he swell with pride over the role he had played in the events of the day? No, there is no trace of cockiness in the men God can trust to lead His battles. If pride is there, it must go!

Elijah sees that the judgments of God have had their effect. A reformation has begun. God will now send rain to refresh the parched land. Yet, not a cloud in sight. But trusting in God's promise, and thoughtful of the king's welfare, Elijah suggests that the monarch go and eat and prepare for rain.

And then the weary prophet, with only his trusted servant, goes to the top of the mountain to pray. Repeatedly he sends his servant to look for some sign of approaching rain. But each time the answer is negative. Elijah prays the more earnestly, searching his own heart. He wonders if some unrecognized sin in his own life could be standing in the way. As he prays, he feels that he himself is nothing and that God is everything. Finally, the seventh time, the servant returns with word that a little cloud, like a man's hand, is rising out of the sea.

That is enough. Elijah doesn't wait for the sky to turn black. He sends his servant to tell Ahab to hurry down the mountain. And then the wind came. And the downpour. And it was getting dark.

The king in his carriage, with the darkness and the blinding rain, could not see his way. And Elijah, who that day had humiliated the king before his people and slain his scheming prophets—Elijah ran ahead of him, down the muddy, slippery slope, to show him the way!

How many of us would be willing to run down a slippery road in the driving rain to show our worst enemy the way?

You say Elijah was a great man that day as he stood fearlessly before his enemies and called down fire from heaven. Yes. But Elijah was never greater than when he, feeling that he himself was nothing, pleaded with God to send the rain. Or when, tired and exhausted as he was, he ran down the slippery mountain to show the king his way!

And friend, the highest, most exalted place that you and I can ever reach is at the foot of an old rugged cross. It is there, feeling that we are nothing and He is everything—it is there that we can see with undimmed vision the power and wonder of Elijah's God. It is there that we can say from a heart made newly clean and forever humble, "O loving Lord, how great Thou art!"

# A Place Called Armageddon

Armageddon! What is it?

To the journalist, it is a convenient term to describe any titanic struggle, military or otherwise. Even a coal strike has been called an "industrial Armageddon."

The author of a religious paperback may confidently describe Armageddon as a decisive and final battle to be fought on a plain in northern Israel, with the Soviet Union, China, and many other nations participating.

To some it is another name for World War III. And others are not sure. They have a vague notion of some devastating nuclear holocaust in which reality will finally outdo the fiction writers.

Armageddon! Frightening! Almost upon us! Breathing the chill of doomsday! But what is it? Does anybody know?

Only about a week after Inauguration Day the president's assistant for national security decided to run a little test. He had been briefed on plans for rescuing the president in the event of an attack on Washington. He wanted to see how it worked.

So Brzezinski called in the old Irishman who had been charged with carrying out such a rescue. With a smile, he asked if he really could get the president out before the missiles came in.

"Yes, sir," the officer answered. "That's why I'm here."

"Have you practiced?" Brzezinski wanted to know.

"Of course!" the officer said proudly. "We test this system all the time."

"That's good, because the president authorized me to do just that." He pushed back his left sleeve and pressed a button on his watch. "Pretend I'm the president. Pretend an alarm has sounded. Get me to safety!"

"Now?" the officer stammered.

"Now!" He pushed the button again. The second hand began its sweep.

The officer protested. "You can't mean now. It's dark. It's snowing. It's—"

He was cut short with a look that stunned him. He babbled a series of breathless orders into the phone.

Brzezinski then dashed for the helicopter rendezvous on the back lawn of the White House. He paused in the outer office only long enough to pick up a secretary to play the role of the first lady.

Then they waited on the back lawn. And waited. Three minutes. Five minutes. Finally the helicopter, which supposedly was always hovering on the alert, dropped down to rescue them.

When at last they were airborne, Brzezinski began testing communications. "Call the joint chiefs," he ordered. And the crewman put the call through the White House switchboard.

"Don't bother to continue. You just flunked communications. If this were really an attack the White House switchboard would be demolished by now."

So it went. It took twice the allotted time to reach the big jet that is supposed to whisk the president away to safety. Known as the doomsday plane, it is a giant 747, elaborately equipped and windowless. It is supposed to be constantly on the alert and ready to take off in three minutes. It wasn't!

One thing more. This little test could easily have been Mr. Brzezinski's last flight. For the officer who had been in charge of the operation for years was so unnerved by having to demonstrate without previous warning that he forgot to give the code words that would let the Secret Service know that the escape helicopter was OK. It was almost shot down as an intruder!

The newspaper article from which I took this little story was entitled "Cruising to Armageddon."

But whatever Armageddon is, it would appear that we aren't quite ready for it!

According to the magazine *Science 80,* it is not simply an attack on Washington, not a single nuclear blast that we have to fear. It raises the possibility that an enemy might try to assure the destruction of the United States by targeting 71 of the 119 largest metropolitan areas—all at once!

And *New West* magazine details the possibility of space wars in our future. Ever since the launching of *Sputnik I,* it says, man-made satellites have been preparing for a silent war in the skies. The superpower that achieves supremacy in space has, of course, an ideal platform from which to direct a war on earth. Not only that. We will soon be able to destroy each other's satellites with laser beams. And the Space Shuttle will be able to place mines on enemy satellites—or even to capture them.

Is it any wonder that we are suffering from what has been called "disastermania"? Disaster books are everywhere. And the evidence is that the books are not the cause of our fear, but rather a reflection of it.

Nuclear war. Terrorists. Crime in the streets. Fires and floods, tornadoes and earthquakes. Crashing planes. And now we have to add volcanoes to the list. We never took volcanoes seriously until Mount St. Helens. But now we do!

So what is this ultimate horror that will finally do this planet in? What is Armageddon? We must turn to Scripture for the answer. For the word has its origin in the book of Revelation. And even there it is used only once. This is what it says: "For they are the spirits of devils, working miracles, which go forth unto the kings of the earth and of the whole world, to gather them to the battle of that great day of God Almighty. . . . And he gathered them together into a place called in the Hebrew tongue Armageddon." Revelation 16:14-16.

Notice that Armageddon is a battle—evidently the final battle in this world's history, for it is called "the battle of that great day of God Almighty." And evidently it is a worldwide conflict, for the nations of all the world are involved.

"A place called in the Hebrew tongue Armageddon." And right here the questions begin. Right here we are confronted with details that we do not know. For in all the world there is no place called Armageddon.

We are told that the place is called Armageddon in the Hebrew tongue. So we turn to the Hebrew for the meaning of the word. And we find that it is a combination of *har,* which means mountain, and *mageddon,* which many have connected with Megiddo, a city of Old Testament times which is now only a ruin hill. So actually, in Hebrew, the name Armageddon is literally "mountain of Megiddo." But nowhere is there a mountain called Megiddo.

It is true that the valley of Megiddo, or the Plain of Esdraelon, has a long history of military conflict. But are we to believe that the armies of all the world could be crowded into the valley of Megiddo in northern Israel?

And that is not all. For other armies, too, are involved. Listen to this: "These [nations] shall make war with the Lamb [Christ], and the Lamb shall overcome them: for he is Lord of lords, and King of kings." Revelation 17:14.

And then this: "The armies which were in heaven followed him [Christ] upon white horses, clothed in fine linen, white and clean." Revelation 19:14.

So the armies of heaven are involved in this battle as well as the armies of earth. The nations may only be fighting each other at first. It may start that way, as a military and political conflict. But ultimately the nations will be fighting against Christ and the armies of heaven. Ultimately this final battle will be an all-out showdown between God and His enemies. And certainly the little valley of Megiddo would be too small for that. It will rapidly escalate into a conflict involving the whole world—and heaven too!

Now here is something that may help us to understand. Sometimes, as we are all aware, a word has more than one meaning. This is the case with the Greek word *topos,* which has been translated "place"—"a place called . . . Armageddon." This Greek word is used, not only to mean a geographical location, but also to mean status, condition, or situation.

Haven't you used the word "place" that way? You've said, "That was a hard place to be in." Or, "I was in a tough place." And you weren't talking about a geographical location at all.

A situation called Armageddon. That makes it easier to understand, doesn't it?

But now, if that is the case, why "mountain of Megiddo"? Why even the hint of a geographical location if it is a *situation* that is referred to?

It is here that the name becomes very interesting and takes on real meaning.

Suppose, if you will, that you wished to visit the ruins of ancient Megiddo. You might take a bus eastward from the port city of Haifa and follow the Carmel ridge, whose western end drops suddenly into the Mediterranean at Haifa. Tell el-Mutesellim, the site of ancient Megiddo, stands at the foot of this ridge on its northeastern edge. And if you were to observe the tell (an ancient ruin) close to the mountain, it would be easy to see why many have identified the mountain of Megiddo with the Carmel ridge. For there, looming large before you as you stand on the Megiddo mound, would be Mount Carmel. And you know what happened atop Mount Carmel!

Yes, in the days of Elijah, on Mount Carmel, the site of one of the great showdowns between God and His enemies. It was there that fire came down from heaven to demonstrate once and for all who was the true God. And the confrontation on Mount Carmel was, in many ways, a miniature of the great showdown to come in the final day.

It is not surprising that God should borrow a symbolism from Old Testament times to help us understand the nature of the conflict that is soon to burst upon us. It is not surprising that He should take a decisive confrontation such as Carmel and make it a symbol of the still more decisive confrontation still to come. For the book of Revelation is a book of symbols, of figures that represent people and situations and last-day events that are very literal.

For instance, let's go back now to verse 12 of this sixteenth chapter, just a few verses before the mention of Armageddon. And we read, "And the sixth angel poured out his vial upon the great river Euphrates; and the water thereof was dried up, that the way of the kings of the east might be prepared." Revelation 16:12.

In this sixteenth chapter we are told of the seven frightful judgments that God will release upon His enemies at the very last. Striking similarities exist between these seven judgments and the ten plagues of Egypt, such as the water turned to blood, the boils, the darkness, and the hail. Why ten judgments were released upon Egypt and only seven at the last we are not told. But the number seven is often used to denote completeness. And certainly, as you look over the account of these final horrors, you will agree that seven is enough!

Another similarity stands out. At the last, as in Egypt, God will make a difference between those who serve Him and those who serve Him not. Just as the Hebrews were untouched, so the child of God today is promised, "A thousand shall fall at thy side, and ten thousand at thy right hand; but it shall not come nigh thee. Only with thine eyes shalt thou behold and see the reward of the wicked. Because thou hast made the Lord, which is my refuge, even the most High, thy habitation; there shall no evil befall thee, neither shall any plague come nigh thy dwelling. For he shall give his angels charge over thee, to keep thee in all thy ways." Psalm 91:7-11.

It is during the sixth, the next to the last of these final judgments, that Armageddon begins. Armageddon continues during the seventh judgment, the battle to be interrupted by the return of Christ.

But back to our scripture. The river Euphrates, mentioned in verse 12, is the river that once ran through the ancient city of Babylon. It is the river of Babylon. Babylon has long since been destroyed. But in the book of Revelation its name is used as the symbol of false worship. Since Babylon here is symbolic, its river must also be symbolic. And its drying up must also be figurative, representing peoples (Revelation 17:15) and the drying up or removal of their support for Babylon, leading to its downfall.

Then to verse 13: "I saw three unclean spirits like frogs come out of the mouth of the dragon, and out of the mouth of the beast, and out of the mouth of the false prophet." Revelation 16:13.

And then to the verse that we read before—verse 14: "For they are the spirits of devils, working miracles, which go forth unto the kings of the earth and of the whole world, to gather them to the battle of that great day of God Almighty."

"Three unclean spirits like frogs." Now certainly the frogs here are not literal—in fact they are plainly said to be unclean spirits, spirits of devils. And certainly the prophecy here is not concerned with a literal dragon or a literal beast. A dragon is often used to represent Satan or a power through which he works. And a beast is often used to represent a nation. The dragon and the beast and the false prophet here are used to represent a threefold coalition of God's enemies—the dragon denoting paganism, the beast denoting a religious and political power that challenges God's law, and the false prophet denoting churches once loyal to God that have fallen away from that loyalty.

Now if Babylon here is figurative, the river is figurative, the frogs are figurative, and the beast and the dragon and the false prophet are figurative, would it be any surprise that God should give this final battle a figurative name? And since Babylon represents false worship all around the world and the Euphrates represents people all around the world—since we are plainly told that all the nations of the world are involved, as well as the armies of heaven—must not the battle of Armageddon be worldwide? We can hardly reach any other conclusion. It would hardly be wise, then, to try to limit it to some exact location in the Middle East.

And right here let me say this. It would be a mistake, a fatal mistake, to suppose that Armageddon, because of all these symbols, is not a literal battle. For certainly it is. God, in order to protect the prophecies of Revelation from His enemies, has made a liberal use of symbols. If His enemies were clearly named and their activities clearly delineated, certainly they would be stirred to destroy the Book.

But the battle of Armageddon will be very, very real. There will be bloodshed beyond anything we can imagine. The large majority of those living on this planet will be slain. Says the prophet Jeremiah, speaking of the same time, "The slain of the Lord shall be at that day from one end of the earth even unto the other end of the earth: they shall not be lamented, neither gathered, nor buried." Jeremiah 25:33.

And those words are not symbolic at all. They are very, very literal!

Yes, only those who have accepted the sacrifice of Jesus, His death in our place, will be spared. That sacrifice was made for all. It is free to all. But unfortunately most will reject it. They refuse His mercy.

You say it is out of character for Jesus, the gentle and compassionate Healer, to destroy? Yes, it is out of character. It is His strange act, the act that He puts off as long as He can. But haven't we asked, again and again, why He doesn't step in and set things right? And how else can He remove evil except by removing those who insist on remaining the perpetrators of evil?

But now notice. The three unclean spirits like frogs are said to be spirits of devils. It is these spirits of devils who lead the nations into Armageddon. It is not simply evil in the hearts of men, corruption even in the highest circles, that is leading the world to ruin. Demon activity is also responsible for what is happening all around us.

I need not tell you that spiritism, in its seemingly limitless forms, is sweeping the world today. This generation seems to be obsessed with the psychic, with the occult. Satan worship has come out into the open. But Satan and his demon helpers also work subtly, under cover, under a thousand unsuspected labels.

Spiritism is spreading like wildfire. It is even infiltrating many of the churches. And this should be no surprise, for we are told that Babylon, the symbol of false worship, has become the refuge of demons. "Babylon the great is fallen, is fallen, and is become the habitation of devils, and the hold of every foul spirit, and a cage of every unclean and hateful bird." Revelation 18:2.

It is no wonder that God makes the urgent plea, "Come out of her, my people, that ye be not partakers of her sins, and that ye receive not her plagues." Verse 4.

But now notice that these demons, these spirits of devils, are able to work miracles. Largely through these miracles the nations are deceived and led into the battle. And these miracles, the work of demons, will be very convincing. We are told that an agent of Satan will even bring down fire from heaven to convince those who look on. "He doeth great wonders, so that he maketh fire come down from heaven on the earth in the sight of men, and deceiveth them that dwell on the earth by the means of those miracles which he had power to do." Revelation 13:13, 14.

Do you see the danger? In the days of Elijah the *supernatural fire was an evidence of the true God.* But it will not be so in the future, for *God will permit Satan to duplicate that miracle.*

Someone says, "Fire from heaven! Then are people to blame if they are deceived? If fire from heaven was solid evidence at Carmel, why isn't it solid evidence in the days that lead to Armageddon? Aren't we at the mercy of deception if fire from heaven is a proof at one time and not at another?"

But I ask you, If God has plainly warned us and if the warning has been written down for centuries for all to see—then are we at the mercy of deception? Have we no defense against the miracles of demons?

To be sure, we walk on dangerous ground these days. Every step we take is on ground that is mined by the enemy. But God's Word is our warning and our defense. Our peril is in neglecting it. To live in the days of Revelation without reading and understanding Revelation is like presuming to operate a high-powered and unfamiliar machine without bothering to read the instructions!

It is easy to say, "I'll be OK. I'll figure it out. I'll just play it by ear." But playing it by ear is dangerous business in an hour like this!

Yes, friend, only as we keep close to God's Word, only as we read and heed its warnings, are we safe from deception. There is no safety—anywhere. To neglect it does not make us sophisticated. It makes us gullible!

The frogs? The unclean spirits like frogs? We cannot be sure just why the frogs are mentioned. Possibly it is because the false doctrines that come out of the mouth of the dragon and the beast and the false prophet are as repulsive to God as slimy frogs might be to us. Remember, too, that in Egypt the frog was considered sacred. And today there are millions who consider sacred the doctrines of devils, spoken by the dragon and the beast and the false prophet.

Remember, too, that in Egypt the magicians were able to produce frogs—at least they appeared to produce them. But they could not remove them. The frogs marked the limit of their power. The three unclean spirits, too, in the days approaching Armageddon, will reach the limit of their power. The mask will be torn away, and they will be exposed as the repulsive masqueraders they are. Too late the deluded millions will see that they have been following demons while professing to follow Christ.

Much that this generation has considered sacred will soon be unmasked and exposed as worthless. Just as the gods of Egypt were helpless to save their worshipers, just as Baal, the sun-god, had no power to vindicate the false and frenzied prophets on Carmel, just so the gods of this generation will soon be exposed as helpless to solve our problem. For too long we have trusted the gods of technology. For too long we have worshiped the gods of chance, the gods of slow, evolutionary change, instead of the God who made heaven and earth. But technology has failed us. The progress we counted on is fast slipping away. The atom has burned our hands. What is left now is the fear—the fear that Jesus told us would be ours. "Men's hearts failing them for fear, and for looking after those things which are coming on the earth." Luke 21:26.

Yes, we are approaching the final showdown. The conflict is accelerating all about us. We can feel it in the air. The participants are still the same as when rebellion first disrupted the peace and harmony of heaven. It is a war between Christ and His angels and Satan and his angels. But now every inhabitant of this planet is to be involved, enlisted on one side or the other.

The issues, too, are the same. Nothing has changed. In Armageddon, as in the showdowns in Egypt and at Mount Carmel, it is the authority of God that is challenged. His government and His law are still the target of the enemy's wrath. Revelation 12:17 tells us that Satan is still angry with God's people—angry because they still insist on keeping the commandments of God.

And sun worship? Sun worship was an issue in the confrontation on the Nile. It was the big issue at Mount Carmel. And believe it or not, it will still be an issue for you and me. Loving obedience has always been the mark of allegiance to God. But Satan, through willing accomplices, will yet take a pagan holiday, a day dedicated to the worship of the sun, and make it a mark of allegiance to himself. And every man and woman and youth will have to choose. Sun worship is not dead!

But thank God, we know the outcome of it all. The nations will fight against Jesus, the Lamb of God, who gave His life for the sins of all the world. And against those on earth who remain loyal to Jesus. Evil men, urged on by demons, will fight against Him who wanted to save them and His representatives, those who "keep the commandments of God, and the faith of Jesus." Revelation 14:12. The battle will be fierce. But the Lamb will overcome!

Just as the people, in the valley of Megiddo, turned their weapons against the priests of Baal who had so long deceived them, just so, before the final battle is over, the disguises will all be torn away. The people, again, will turn their weapons against the false prophets who have so ruthlessly deluded them. And the battle, at last, will be over!

Yes, friend, if you take a peek at the back of the Book, you'll see that Jesus wins! And He will win at the last because He won on that dark Friday when He died, alone and forsaken, on a rough and rugged cross outside Jerusalem!

It is to that cross, to the suffering Lamb of God who died there, that we now turn our eyes. It is to Golgotha's splintery cross that I invite you to nail your colors and declare your loyalty.

But there is so little time. Already we hear in the distance the sounds of the final battle. And when Armageddon has slipped out of the future and into the past, only one question will matter. What have you done with the Lamb?

# Showdown at Golgotha

It happened on a Friday. It happened in the sensitive, unpredictable, explosive Middle East. On the surface it appeared to be nothing more than a routine execution of three criminals on a hill outside Jerusalem. And Rome was using its favorite means of torture and shame and death—crucifixion.

All nature seemed to be offended by what was taking place. The sun refused to shine on the scene. The earth quaked. Lightning bolts took close aim. All nature seemed to know what men did not. A rebel planet had just crucified its Creator!

The crucifixion of Jesus of Nazareth is the most irrational fact of all history. It seems to make no sense at all. Jesus was the only perfect Man who ever lived. No trace of weakness or selfishness or pride, no wrong of any kind, was ever found in Him. His enemies would have paid any price for evidence that would condemn Him. But they were forced to employ false witnesses whose testimony was conflicting, contradictory, and obviously hired. Pilate had tried Him, found Him guiltless, and wanted to free Him. But conscience had been overridden by political pressure.

So it was that the one perfect Man died at the hands of His own people!

Was He, then, simply the helpless victim of jealous enemies? Victim, yes. But certainly not a helpless victim. Again and again He had foiled their attempts to take Him. Repeatedly He had walked through the crowd and escaped unharmed.

Only the night before, as they had come to arrest Him, divinity had flashed through His countenance, an angel had passed between Him and the mob, and they had fallen as dead men. Easily He could have walked away. Instead, He had permitted them to bind Him, torture Him, try Him, condemn Him, and crucify Him. But He was hardly a helpless victim. He who could have called ten thousand angels to His side was dying without protest. He was dying of His own choice—not as a suicide, but as a sacrifice!

He had said in the hearing of His enemies, "The reason my Father loves me is that I lay down my life—only to take it up again. No one takes it from me, but I lay it down of my own accord." John 10:17, 18, N.I.V.

Throughout His ministry Jesus had been in constant conflict with the religious leaders of His day. In the first place, they were unhappy with this brilliant young Teacher because He had not attended one of their schools. He was in no way a product of their teaching. They looked for the promised Messiah, but they expected the Messiah to come with the pomp and glory of a king. They were not ready to accept this humble and unpretentious Teacher.

Not only that. Jesus had often exposed their hypocrisy. He had a way of telling little stories and asking them to comment. And often in their response they condemned themselves before they realized that they were the culprits in the story. His healing was making Him more and more popular with the people. His love and compassion stood out in bold contrast to their own rigid, uncaring attitudes. Their influence was endangered. They were losing their control of the people. Something must be done. Jesus must be eliminated.

A final clash was inevitable. And now it had come. They had succeeded in removing the One who had threatened their power and influence. Jesus lay dead in Joseph's tomb.

Yet it had been a strange confrontation—a conflict in which one of the contestants seemed not to be fighting at all. Jesus seemed to be passively submitting to defeat without protest.

And defeat is exactly what it seemed to be. The disciples of Jesus were crushed. They had truly believed Him to be the Messiah, the Son of God. But now He was dead. And surely the Son of God could not die. They must have made a mistake.

As for the enemies of Jesus, His death did not bring them the satisfaction they had expected. Hadn't He said that He had power to lay down His life and take it up again? What if He should do just that? They feared the dead Christ far more than they had feared the living Christ. They were terrified at the thought that He might suddenly confront them on the street, or even in the privacy of home, and call them to account for what they had done.

And yet everything about the crucifixion of Jesus seemed to spell defeat. Jesus, who claimed to be the Son of God, was dead. The cross at Golgotha was like a giant bulletin board announcing the failure of Jesus of Nazareth, the end of all His claims.

But the truth is that Calvary was not an accident. Not the premature end of a promising career. The cross of Calvary was intended. Jesus came to be crucified.

That's why He came! In death He was victor.

Calvary was not a defeat. It was the greatest success of all time. It was a success, an achievement, an accomplishment that made heaven ring with song!

Calvary was the most critical showdown of all history. And Jesus had not been defeated. He had won. Yet not one human being, as they watched beside the cross that dark Friday—not one understood what was happening!

You see, the real showdown that day was not with the jealous enemies of Jesus. It was not with Rome. It was not with those who drove the nails. The real showdown was with an invisible enemy. The fate of the whole human race trembled in the balance as the conflict with the unseen foe reached its climax. For the outcome would affect the destiny of this planet and every person on it!

Is it difficult for you to think of the life of Jesus as in any sense a showdown? Jesus, who went about healing the sick, comforting and cheering the despondent, offering hope to all who would receive it? Jesus, who left protest and revolution to others, and quietly talked about love and forgiveness and going the second mile?

Of course His teaching of love and forgiveness, and His personal demonstration of that which He taught, must have seemed like lunacy in a culture so known for its violence. And it put Him in constant conflict with the religious leaders of His people. That was only the visible conflict, hardly thought of as a showdown even by His closest friends.

Little did any human observer sense what was really happening. It was only Jesus Himself who understood the desperate controversy that swirled about Him, silently and unseen, all through His life.

He Himself had understood it clearly since He was twelve years old. For it was then that He visited the magnificent temple in Jerusalem and watched the white-robed priests performing their duties. He saw them placing innocent lambs upon the altar of sacrifice. He knew that the blood of animals could never take away sin. There must be a better sacrifice. And then the secret of His own mission opened to His keen young mind. He knew now why He had come to this planet. He—Himself—He was to be the Lamb!

And from that moment He never allowed His feet to be diverted from the path to Golgotha!

The truth is that Jesus had understood His mission long before Bethlehem. For it was in those days, when He was one with the Father, when His was the worship and adoration of angels—it was then that His decision had been made. It was then, when man first sinned, that He offered to be man's Saviour. The book of Revelation speaks of Him as "the Lamb slain from the foundation of the world." Revelation 13:8.

Yes, Jesus knew what was going on. So did His Father. So did the angels. And so did the watching worlds.

And Satan, the rebel angel who desperately wanted the place of the Son of God, who was determined to overthrow the very throne of God—he knew what the controversy was all about. And every one of his demons knew.

When the fallen angel saw the beautiful planet that God had fitted up as a home for our first parents, he determined to destroy it all. He knew that he himself, with his rebel angels, was headed for destruction. He determined to take the human race with him.

It looked easy when Adam and Eve so quickly forsook their allegiance to God. Satan determined to make this planet the headquarters of rebellion. He didn't think God would bother with one little planet and one man and woman. Surely they would just be written off. He couldn't believe that God Himself would actually come down to this earth to challenge his rebellion. He had charged God with not caring for His subjects, with being a stranger to love and compassion. He claimed that it was he, Lucifer, who had the interest of the angels at heart. Not only had the government of God been challenged, but the very character of God had been called in question.

Little did the fallen angel know that he was dealing with One in whose heart Calvary lay hidden. Little did he dream that one day, on a hill called Golgotha, there would be a showdown. And all the universe would see who it was who cared!

Satan, in the Garden of Eden, heard the first promise of a Saviour and pondered what the words might mean. He watched the sacrifice of lambs and tried to understand the significance of it all. He turned to the Scriptures, and of course, with the brilliant mind of an angel, he was not a dull student. He was convinced that the Son of God Himself was coming to this earth to challenge his authority and break his hold upon the human race. He determined that the mission of mercy to fallen men and women should never be carried out.

Satan saw the light over Bethlehem and heard the glad song of the angels. He trembled at what it meant. He tried to destroy Jesus as a baby. But failing in that, he awaited the opportune moment for a head-on confrontation.

When Jesus was baptized in the Jordan and retired to the wilderness to pray, the time seemed right. Jesus, hungry and alone, was now at His weakest. Adam and

Eve had fallen so easily. Surely Jesus, with humanity upon Him, with a body weakened by four thousand years of sin in His human ancestry—surely Jesus now would be an easy mark.

He appeared to Jesus first in the guise of a brilliant angel. Surely, the tempter suggested, the Son of God would not be left, hungry and alone and forsaken, in the wilderness. Was He really the Son of God? Was He sure? If He was, why didn't He turn those desert stones to bread? And the temptation, the urge to prove His identity, was strong. But Jesus said, "It is written, Man shall not live by bread alone, but by every word that proceedeth out of the mouth of God." Matthew 4:4.

Then, after another try, Satan dropped his mask and attempted to make a deal with Jesus. "If You will just worship me—fall down and worship me just once, worship me just a little—I will call off the controversy. It will all be over. You won't have to walk the bloodstained path to a shameful death."

And again the temptation was intense—the temptation to compromise, to make a deal, to take a shortcut, to have the controversy finished. But Jesus said with a clear note of finality, "Get thee hence, Satan: for it is written, Thou shalt worship the Lord thy God, and him only shalt thou serve." Matthew 4:10.

And Satan, when commanded by the Son of God to leave, dared not resist. He retired from the conflict, writhing in anger and defeat. From then on he hounded the steps of Jesus all the way to the cross.

Satan, at Golgotha, stirred up the mob to taunt the Son of God in His dying agony. Satan instigated the abuse and the torture. It was he who had fired the mob to cry, "Crucify Him!"

But Satan didn't really want Jesus to die. He only

wanted to keep Jesus from going through with His plan. He knew that if he took the life of his own Creator he would have no sympathy left anywhere in the universe. But he felt certain that if he just made it hard enough, horrible enough, shameful enough, Jesus would come down from the cross and abandon His plan to save men. He would let them die for their own sins.

But it didn't work out that way. And when Jesus drew His last breath, Satan knew that he was doomed!

The controversy is not over yet. The forces of good and evil are still contending for the control of men and women—one to save, and the other to destroy. The conflict will be settled in the great battle of Armageddon. But it is also being settled in the minds and hearts of individuals, including you and me. For it is not territory that Satan wants. It is worship!

The issues in the conflict are still the same. The authority of God is still challenged, along with His character and His government and His law.

Lucifer, in heaven, at the beginning of his rebellion, demanded that God's law be dispensed with. But Golgotha was God's final answer. For the cross of Calvary says loud and clear, "No! The law cannot be pushed aside and ignored or changed. The law, which is a description of the character of God, must stand. The law, when broken, demands the death of the sinner. There was no way to save the sinner except for the Son of God to die in the sinner's place. The law could not be changed even to save the life of God's own Son. If it could be altered or set aside, then Jesus need not have died. If it could be bypassed, even once, then Calvary was only a meaningless drama!"

That is the unmistakable message of the cross. But Satan today, as truly as in the days of Elijah, is still trying to turn men away from the commandments of God. And today, cunning deceiver that he is, he boldly suggests that the cross has somehow made the law inoperative. He tries to make the cross a weapon against the government and law of God!

The enemy, when Adam fell, charged that God's law was unreasonable, that it could not be kept by humanity. But Jesus kept it. And now the fallen angel charges that no one else can really keep it. And the answer to his charge must come in the transformed lives of men and women like you and me.

How often we have embarrassed our Lord! How often we have given Satan the opportunity to say to the Saviour, "Yes, You can forgive them. You can forgive them over and over. But You can't give them the power to stop sinning! You can't really change them!"

Thank God it isn't true! Thank God that Calvary can do more about sin than forgive it! For He who supplies the pardon can also supply the power!

The showdown at Golgotha was over the character of God. The showdown today is over the character of men and women. Can God give us both the pardon and the power?

Long ago a woman, accused and guilty, was brought into the presence of Jesus as He was teaching. What should be done with her? She waited in terror for someone to cast the first stone. But Jesus wrote in the dust at His feet the sins of her accusers, and one by one they silently slipped away.

Then Jesus said to the trembling one, "Neither do I condemn you. Go and sin no more!"

And in His words was the power to do as He commanded. In His words was *the power to go and sin no more!*

That, friend, is the message of Golgotha. Whoever you are, no matter how badly you have tangled the threads of life, the Lord Jesus offers you pardon. And He offers you *the power to go and sin no more.*

"Rock of Ages, cleft for me,
Let me hide myself in Thee;
Let the water and the blood,
From Thy riven side which flowed,
Be of sin the double cure,
Clease me from its guilt and power."

Yes, Golgotha's cross is a double cure. It can save us, if we are willing, from both the guilt and the power of sin.

When God brought His people out of Egypt, He was reminding us of His ability to deliver us from the enemy's control. It was Calvary that broke the *power* of sin. And when the guns of Armageddon are finally silenced by the appearing of the Lord Jesus Christ in the blazing skies, then our Lord will deliver us from the *presence* of sin. He will rescue us from this troubled world even as He led His people out of ancient Egypt. He will say to this rebel planet, "Let My people go!" And no power on earth will dare resist! Nor will any power be able.

Friend, is the blood on your doorpost? Will the destroying angel pass over your home? Will Jesus, the Rock of Ages, be your refuge when the burning falls? Will you be ready and willing, at a moment's notice, to break the hold of this world upon your affections—and follow Jesus home?

Many a conflict has been decided in the explosive Middle East. But the controversy now has moved into your heart and mine, to be decided, without force or coercion, in the sensitive and sacred precincts of the soul. What will be your choice? How will the conflict within be settled?

If you take a peek at the back of the Book, Jesus wins! But will a peek at your inner heart send heaven into a riot of song? Will Jesus win there too? It's a showdown that you alone can resolve. And there's so little time!

# SHOWDOWN IN THE MIDDLE EAST

## George E. Vandeman

**The Middle East! Bloodshed, intrigue, oil! The crossroads of the world! Christians, Muslims, and Jews! All see their destiny in this ancient land.**

**No place on earth seems to be more explosive today. Some say that Armageddon, earth's last battle, will be fought in the Middle East.**

**Above all the earthly conflicts for this fabled land are the great showdowns that God has had with those who have opposed His purposes and His designated people—all focusing in the Middle East!**

**In this book George Vandeman brings his readers face to face with earth's last showdown. Everyone will be involved. No one can evade the coming showdown.**

**George Vandeman, speaker of It Is Written telecast, writes as he speaks. His books have sold more than seven million copies. Freshness and warmth carry his message to the head and heart. Readers are never again the same.**

**ISBN 0-8163-0392-4**